Instant Responsive Web Design

Learn the important components of responsive web design and make your websites mobile-friendly

Cory Simmons

BIRMINGHAM - MUMBAI

Instant Responsive Web Design

First published: September 2013

Production Reference: 1230913

Published by Packt Publishing Ltd.
Livery Place
35 Livery Street
Birmingham B3 2PB, UK.

ISBN 978-1-84969-925-9

www.packtpub.com

Credits

Author

Cory Simmons

Reviewers

Dario Calonaci

Matt Rheault

Acquisition Editor

Kevin M. Colaco

Commissioning Editor

Priyanka Shah

Technical Editor

Vivek Pillai

Project Coordinator

Michelle Quadros

Proofreader

Hardip Sidhu

Production Coordinator

Kyle Albuquerque

Cover Work

Kyle Albuquerque

Cover Image

Ronak Dhruv

About the Author

Cory Simmons is a web designer/developer with over 17 years of experience. He currently works at Pressed Web, where he has maintained a tutorial blog for years covering everything from basic HTML/CSS to Django and Meteor. He has worked for companies such as Scholastic and World Vision Charities. Cory has written for CSS Tricks and is an author at TutsPlus. He created and maintains the Jeet Framework.

About the Reviewers

Dario Calonaci is a Graphic Designer who has specialized in Typography and Logo Design.

He has worked for the United Nations conference *Rio+20*, selected for *Obama for America* and *Node.js*. His name and work appears on a book presentation inside the Senate's Library in Rome. He has been teaching Web Design since he was 23 years old. He is also a member of FacultyRow, a NY based association as a valuable Teacher and Academic figure.

He has been invited to talk at two seminars and run one workshop; his works have also been published internationally. He has also studied in a couple of thesis.

You may know more about him in his website `http://dariocalonaci.com`.

Matt Rheault likes to design and create things on the web. He enjoys his morning cup of coffee and the satisfaction of getting the job done. He specializes in full website, e-commerce, blog, and responsive web app development. His roots are in graphic and UI design, however he has extensive back and front-end development experience to ensure that he can create a full-fledged product from start to finish. When he is not at his desk working, you can usually find him cooking up some bacon or hanging out with his vegetarian girlfriend—oh the irony!

Check out his personal website at `mattrheault.com`, and his company website at `fueled4.com`.

www.packtpub.com

Support files, eBooks, discount offers and more

You might want to visit www.packtpub.com for support files and downloads related to your book.

Did you know that Packt offers eBook versions of every book published, with PDF and ePub files available? You can upgrade to the eBook version at www.packtpub.com and as a print book customer, you are entitled to a discount on the eBook copy. Get in touch with us at service@packtpub.com for more details.

At www.packtpub.com, you can also read a collection of free technical articles, sign up for a range of free newsletters and receive exclusive discounts and offers on Packt books and eBooks.

packtlib.packtpub.com

Do you need instant solutions to your IT questions? PacktLib is Packt's online digital book library. Here, you can access, read and search across Packt's entire library of books.

Why Subscribe?

- ✦ Fully searchable across every book published by Packt
- ✦ Copy and paste, print and bookmark content
- ✦ On demand and accessible via web browser

Free Access for Packt account holders

If you have an account with Packt at www.packtpub.com, you can use this to access PacktLib today and view nine entirely free books. Simply use your login credentials for immediate access.

Table of Contents

Instant Responsive Web Design

Welcome to *Instant Responsive Web Design*. This book was written to provide you with all the information you need to start building responsive, mobile-friendly websites today.

You will learn various strategies for making your websites behave appropriately on every device with a minimal amount of additional work.

This book contains the following sections:

So, what is Responsive Web Design (RWD)? helps you discover why RWD is such an important tool in your web design arsenal.

Getting started will help you acquire the tools necessary to start designing your first responsive website.

Quick start – making your first responsive web page will help you to make a responsive web page using CSS media queries.

Top 5 Features you need to know about will help you to build responsive websites on your own. The features we'll cover are the power of CSS Media Queries, different strategies to make responsive websites, desktop-first versus mobile-first, gotchas and best practices, and putting it all together.

People and places you should get to know explains that RWD is more of a technique than a community-driven project, but even so there are some important contributors you should follow for fresh, creative solutions to problems with RWD. In this section I'll introduce you to them and let you know about some great places you can go to learn more about RWD and get help in case you get lost.

So, what is Responsive web design (RWD)?

Responsive web design (**RWD**) is the practice of making a website's layout change depending on what device and/or resolution the website is being viewed on. For instance, you may have a navigation bar at the top of your website with links laid out in a horizontal manner when viewed on desktop monitors, but when viewed on a small cell phone screen, wouldn't it be better if those links stacked on top of each other or collapsed into a menu?

This kind of thinking is what separates good web designers from great web designers, and the best part is, it's incredibly easy to up your game with a little bit of knowledge. When you are competing at job interviews or for a prospective client, who is more likely to get the job? The person who knows how to make websites, or the person who knows how to make websites that act great on any device? It's always a huge advantage to be the person who can tap into the ever growing landscape of non-desktop users. Clients love that.

So how does it work? With the help of something called CSS Media Queries.

CSS Media Queries are little wrappers in CSS. They appear in three forms. One form appears in your <head> tags and will supply a different stylesheet usually depending on what the width of the viewport is (amongst other conditions), and looks like the following code:

```
<link rel="stylesheet" media="(max-width: 700px)"
  href="mobile.css">
```

[If the maximum size of the viewport is 700 px wide, activate another stylesheet.]

Another form appears as an @import directive in your stylesheet itself and can look something like the following code:

```
@import url(mobile.css) and (max-width: 700px);
```

[Activate a mobile stylesheet when the width of the screen is at most 700 px.]

The most common form of a media query will appear in your stylesheet and looks something like the following code:

```
@media (max-width: 700px) {
    body {
        background: blue;
    }
}
```

 If the maximum width of the page is 700 px wide, change the background color to blue.

In the preceding example, if you click on the edge of your browser and drag it to make the viewport smaller, the background of the entire page will change to blue when you get to and below 700 px. When you expand the viewport above 700 px, it will revert to the default white background. Pretty cool, huh?

`max-width` is just one of the many options you can pass to these media queries to target a myriad of devices and sizes. For instance, you can change the appearance of your website for printers to save your visitors some ink. Or, you can use `min-width` to change the layout of the website as you scale up from a small device. This approach is called the mobile-first approach and is gaining a larger following every day, but we'll get into that later. The point is that media queries are very powerful.

RWD saves an enormous amount of resources and time when making your site device agnostic. Here's why:

+ **One code base**: Imagine having to design and code around four to five websites each time you made a website. It's much easier to design one site and simply rearrange elements to fit whatever device they're on.

+ **Work harder, make more money**: This one applies to the client and the designer. Responsive sites are accessible sites; therefore, your clients' websites are reaching more people (which is good for their businesses). Since you're doing more work, you are justified in raising the price a bit.

+ **Past and future proof**: Media queries have been around for several years, so you can be rest assured knowing that all modern browsers and most devices support media queries out of the box. In lieu of every browser supporting media queries, there are great polyfills (JavaScript plugins that add modern functionality to older browsers) like `Respond.js` that will allow you to confidently support almost everyone all the way back to IE6 if you have to target that for some reason. Not only that, but RWD is future proof if done right. This means that the largest or smallest monitors will deliver beautiful, highly-usable websites now and forever.

An example of Responsive web design is how Paravel's (`http://paravelinc.com`)

`Microsoft.com` redesign provides various layouts depending on browser width:

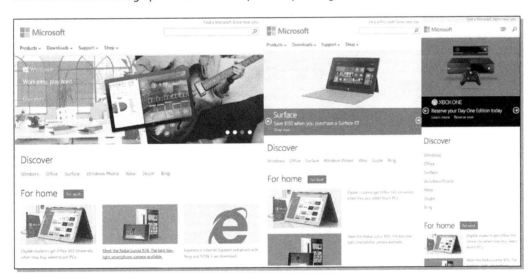

Quite a lot of sites are now responsive. You can check any site by adjusting your browser width, but if you'd just like to see an exceptional list of responsive websites, check out `http://mediaqueri.es` shown as follows:

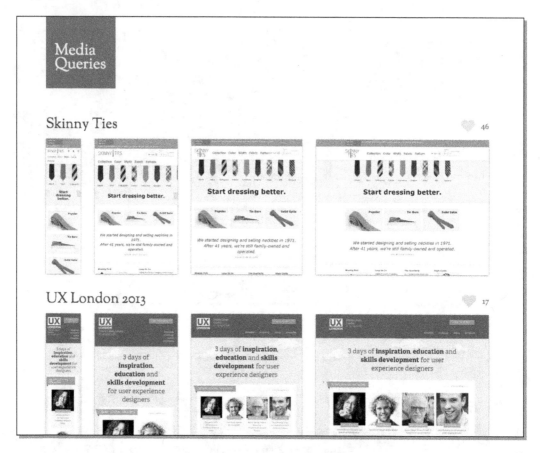

`http://mediaqueri.es` features quite a large list of beautiful and responsive websites.

Media queries and RWD have reinvigorated and revolutionized a somewhat stale industry in web designing. The job of a web designer is no longer to solely make a beautiful site, but now encompasses making a beautiful site that is extremely usable to everyone who may visit it. I think that adds a lot of value to our profession and if you're sitting on the fence about whether or not you should take the time to learn RWD, you better get hip quick because it's quickly becoming the standard.

Getting started

To follow the content of this book, we assume that you have a basic knowledge of how to make websites using HTML and CSS. If you don't know HTML/CSS, you might want to acquire some more Packt Publishing's books and/or look into the online series by *Jeffrey Way*, *Web Development from Scratch* and free video course *30 Days to Learn HTML & CSS*. All of these resources are fantastic. As with anything, getting good with HTML/CSS just takes a lot of practice and actually creating things, so don't be afraid to break things.

If you know basic web development, you probably already have all the tools necessary to get into RWD, but I'm going to point out my two favorites: Sublime Text and Chrome.

Sublime Text is a great little text editor, and Chrome is a lightning fast browser with amazing W3C specification support and a great/built-in set of Developer Tools that will help you realize what is going on with your website. You can purchase Sublime Text if you have the money, but if you don't, you can use it as a free trial forever. Of course, Chrome is free.

Once you have Sublime Text, I highly recommend you to search for Sublime Text Package Control and follow the installation instructions. Once you have it installed, press *Ctrl + Shift + P* (or *cmd + Shift + P* on a Mac) and type in `Package Control: Install Package`, then install Emmet. You can learn more about Emmet at `http://emmet.io`, but suffice to say, it will save you an enormous amount of typing and time.

If these aren't your cup of tea, also check out JetStorm's WebStorm (free trial) and Mozilla Firefox with the Firebug add-on.

```html
01_sublime_text.html                                              01_sublime_text.html

 1  <!DOCTYPE html>
 2  <html>
 3      <head>
 4          <meta charset="utf-8">
 5          <meta http-equiv="X-UA-Compatible" content="IE=edge,chrome=1">
 6          <title>Responsive Web Design</title>
 7          <meta name="viewport" content="width=device-width">
 8          <link rel="stylesheet" href="css/style.css">
 9      </head>
10      <body>
11
12          <header id="h">
13              <div>
14                  <a href="/" id="logo">Logo</a>
15              </div>
16          </header>
17
18          <section>
19              <article>
20                  <header>
21                      <h1>Hello, World</h1>
22                  </header>
23              </article>
24              <p>
25                  Lorem ipsum dolor sit amet, consectetur adipisicing elit. Natus, ipsam, unde reiciendis odit assumenda veniam
                    molestias error aliquid fugiat minima ex placeat voluptatibus harum beatae et obcaecati aperiam vero eos.
26              </p>
27          </section>
28
29          <script src="http://ajax.googleapis.com/ajax/libs/jquery/1.9.0/jquery.min.js"></script>
30      </body>
31  </html>

Line 14, Column 43                                              Spaces: 4         HTML
```

Downloading the color graphics PDF

For downloading the colored graphics of this book visit: http://www.packtpub.com/sites/default/files/downloads/9259OT_ColoredImages.pdf

Sublime Text on the left, Chrome with Developer Tools opened on the right. The perfect combination!

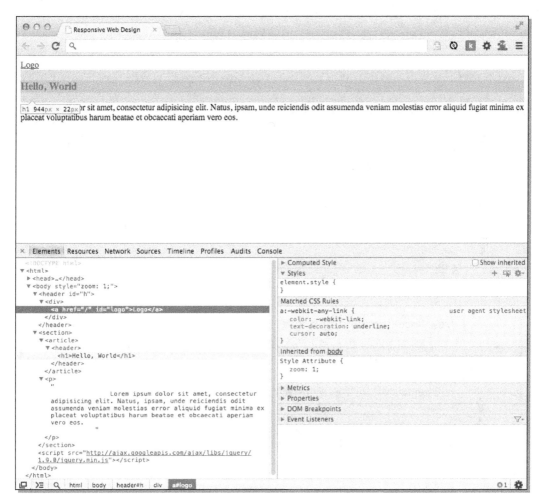

Quick start – making your first responsive web page

In this section we'll get started by creating a simple page and making it responsive.

Step 1 – creating an HTML page

Create a folder on your desktop called `Responsive`. Inside of that, create a file called `playground.html`. Open it up in your favorite editor and open the same file in the browser of your choice (right-click on the file and look for `Open with...`).

Add some boilerplate HTML code to `playground.html` shown as follows:

```html
<html>
    <head>
        <title>Responsive Playground</title>
        <link rel="stylesheet" href="style.css">
    </head>
    <body>

    </body>
</html>
```

Downloading the example code

You can download the example code files for all Packt books you have purchased from your account at `http://www.packtpub.com`. If you purchased this book elsewhere, you can visit `http://www.packtpub.com/support` and register to have the files e-mailed directly to you.

We're creating a very generic web page that links to an external stylesheet to help separate the structure of our site (HTML) from the style (CSS).

Step 2 – adding a stylesheet

Create a file called `style.css` in the same folder and open it in your editor. Add the following code to it just to make sure that it's working properly:

```css
body {
    background: blue;
}
```

We're just setting the background color to blue to make sure the stylesheet is linked to our playground.html page properly.

Now refresh `playground.html` in your browser. Have a look at the following screenshot:

You should notice your page's background is now blue:

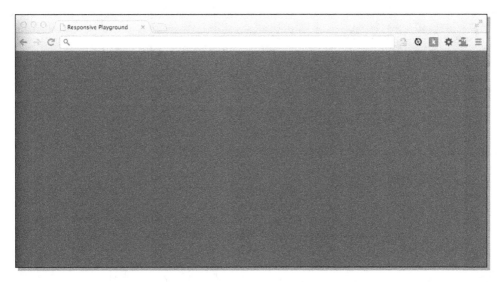

Make sure your browser window isn't maximized; use your mouse to grab the left edge of the browser and shrink it to the right as much as you want, then expand it back to the left. You'll end up doing a lot of this. For brevity, I'll refer to this specific action as contracting and expanding from now on.

So, what happened? Well, we simulated what your site might look like on a generic mobile device, but other than that, nothing changed visually.

Step 3 – making it responsive

Let's wrap our entire `body { ... }` selector with a media query shown as follows:

```
@media (max-width: 700px) {
    body {
        background: blue;
    }
}
```

 The `@media` symbol essentially monitors any changes to the browser's properties and will activate the wrapped CSS when those changes are `True`.

Save your changes and refresh your browser. Now expand and contract your web page. What happens? Well, when the viewport of your browser hits 700 px, your web page should go from white (the default) to blue (our media query).

Congratulations! You just took a huge step towards becoming a RWD master.

But, how often are you actually going to be swapping the background of your design for various devices? Let's create a real-world responsive website complete with:

+ Logo
+ Primary horizontal navigation
+ Sidebar with page-specific navigation
+ Content area
+ Footer with some social media links

Modify your `playground.html` file to include the following code:

```
<!DOCTYPE html>
<html>
    <head>
        <title>Responsive Playground</title>
        <link rel="stylesheet" href="style.css">
    </head>
    <body>
```

```
<header class="top">
    <a href="/" class="logo"><img src="logo.png" alt="RWD
      Logo"></a>
</header>

<nav class="primary">
    <a href="#">Link</a>
    <a href="#">Link</a>
    <a href="#">Link</a>
    <a href="#">Link</a>
</nav>

<div class="main">

    <aside class="sidebar">
        <nav>
            <a href="#">Sublink</a>
            <a href="#">Sublink</a>
            <a href="#">Sublink</a>
        </nav>
    </aside>

    <section class="content">

        <article>
            <header>
                <h1>Hello World</h1>
                <p>
                    Lorem ipsum...
                </p>
            </header>
        </article>

    </section>

</div>

<footer class="bottom">
    <nav>
        <a href="#">Facebook</a>
        <a href="#">YouTube</a>
        <a href="#">Twitter</a>
    </nav>
</footer>

    </body>
</html>
```

We're using semantic (meaningful to search engines and screen readers) HTML5 tags to structure our page. To learn more about HTML5 tags check out HTML5Doctor.com.

Now, replace the code in your `style.css` file with the following code:

```css
* {
    margin: 0;
    padding: 0;
    background: rgba(0,0,0,.05);
}
body {
    width: 980px;
    margin: 20px auto;
    font: 13px/21px Arial, sans-serif;
}
.top {
    overflow: hidden;
    margin-bottom: 20px;
}
.logo img {
    float: left;
    margin-right: 20px;
    height: 100px;
}
nav.primary {
    float: right;
    overflow: hidden;
    margin-top: 35px;
}
nav.primary a {
    float: left;
    padding: 5px 30px;
}
.main {
    overflow: hidden;
    margin-bottom: 20px;
}
.sidebar {
    float: left;
    width: 280px;
    margin-right: 20px;
}
.sidebar a {
    display: block;
    margin-bottom: 10px;
}
.sidebar a:last-child {
```

```
        margin-bottom: 0;
    }
    .content {
        float: left;
        width: 680px;
    }
    p {
        margin-bottom: 20px;
    }
    p:last-of-type {
        margin-bottom: 0;
    }
    h1 {
        font-size: 30px;
        line-height: 1.1;
        margin-bottom: 10px;
    }
    footer {
        overflow: hidden;
    }
    footer a {
        float: left;
        padding: 5px 15px;
    }
```

 This is a very common 980 px wide layout.

Save your files and refresh your browser and you should see something similar to the following screenshot. Did you notice the `*  { background: rgba(0,0,0,.05); }` bit? That little trick is great for prototyping a layout. It helps you visualize all the building blocks of your site.

Now expand and contract your page. What happens? If you're on a big monitor, the margins on the sides of the page will shrink while the layout stays centered, but when the width of the viewport becomes smaller than 980 px, the design is cut off and you get a horizontal scrollbar—not good!

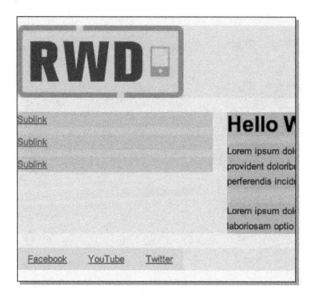

Oh no! It's not responding to devices with smaller viewports. Poor mobile users!

This is called a Fixed layout. It is set for a specific size (and usually centered), but when you view it on a mobile device, it's clipped. We can fix the Fixed layout by providing certain CSS, so when the page falls to 980 px, that will rearrange the layout of the site. This will give all the site's visitors a great experience.

As any good programmer knows that making a checklist helps in organizing their tasks. So, let's make a checklist of things we would like to rearrange:

+ **Logo**: The logo should stack on top of the primary navigation and be centered
+ **Primary Navigation**: Each link should stack on top of each other and span the full width of the page
+ **Secondary Navigation**: For simplicity's sake, we'll just have these links stack on top of each other too
+ **Content area**: Again, let's just stack this content up too
+ **Footer**: Since we're pretty confident this will only be a few links (3), we can just leave them side-by-side, but maybe we should make them span the width of the page so they look nice

Notice anything about our plan? So far, we're just stacking things on top of each other and usually making them full-width elements. Of course you can arrange and rearrange things however you want, but an easy way to make a site phone-friendly is to simply stack elements on top of each other.

But, won't this bore people on mobile devices? No! They are used to sites that deliver a terrible mobile experience and they're typically not browsing websites on their mobile device for the sheer beauty, but rather, they're out with friends at a coffee shop and want to see if their favorite band is playing that night. If they can go to the band's website on their phone, click on their **Gigs** page, and quickly find when the band is playing next, you've done your job as a responsive web designer exceptionally well and you can expect that visitor to come back the next time they're out with friends.

There are definitely things we can do to make the design a bit friendlier (have a **Menu** button that expands the menu rather than wasting screen real-estate by stacking buttons on top of each other on every page), but we'll get into those later. To produce a job that responds quickly, the stack-width approach is an absolute gem.

Without further ado, here is the code that will make your Fixed layout beautifully responsive. You'll need to append this onto the end of your `style.css`:

```css
@media (max-width: 980px) {
    body {
        width: 100%;
        margin: 10px auto;
    }
    .top {
        margin-bottom: 10px;
    }
    .logo {
        display: block;
        text-align: center;
        margin-bottom: 10px;
    }
    .logo img {
        float: none;
        margin-right: 0;
        height: auto;
        width: 30%;
    }
    nav.primary {
        float: none;
        margin-top: 0;
        text-align: center;
    }
    nav.primary a {
        float: none;
        display: block;
```

```
        margin-bottom: 10px;
    }
    nav.primary a:last-child {
        margin-bottom: 0;
    }
    .sidebar {
        float: none;
        width: 100%;
        margin-right: 0;
        margin-bottom: 10px;
        text-align: center;
    }
    .main {
        margin-bottom: 10px;
    }
    .content {
        float: none;
        width: 96%;
        padding: 2%;
    }
    footer a {
        width: 33.333%;
        padding: 5px 0;
        text-align: center;
    }
}
```

 Did you notice how we are making all of these changes within the same media query? The fewer media queries, the fewer times you're rearranging the layout, the better.

Let's save, refresh our browsers, and enjoy our handy work! Voila! We now have a website that looks, and more importantly, functions beautifully on almost every device. Hey! You're pretty good for a beginner! Have a look at the following screenshot:

The layout you get at smaller screen widths

So what did we do exactly? First, we created a wrapper that directs the browser to activate the code when the browser's width gets to and below 980 px. After that, we just started removing floats from things and tweaking the widths and alignments of elements.

See? This stuff isn't that difficult. Don't be afraid of it. You just make a wrapper, contract your viewport, and then start tweaking things until they look good for smaller screens. There're a lot of cool things media queries can do and, as with anything, there are a lot of gotchas that you have to watch out for, but we'll cover all that in the next section. For now, be proud that you have understood the gist of RWD.

Top 5 features you need to know about

In this section we'll learn about some core features you'll need to know in order to be a competent responsive designer. We'll cover technical things like what media queries are, and different approaches you'll need to be comfortable with, to make good decisions on what kind of responsive designer you want to be.

The power of CSS Media Queries

Media queries are the backbone of RWD. In this section we'll get familiar with what they are and what they can do. You'll use them often, but you won't have to memorize everything that they're capable of. It means that you should be familiar with what they can do in case the need ever arises.

Media types

Media queries are no joke. So far you've only learned about `max-width`, but there are seemingly endless ways of targeting various devices. It gets as abstract as writing media queries for braille readers and, get this, the scanning type of projection devices. Finally, you can serve a different batch of CSS for both progressive and interlace TVs!

I'll spare you the possibilities as they're available online if you search for MDN Media Queries and we'll just focus on the media queries you'll actually use.

Firstly, you should know there is a list of media types you can target explicitly. Things like projectors and TVs are supported, but the two you'll mostly work with are `screen` and `print`. In fact, you'll mostly target `print` explicitly, and that's just if you feel like your content will be frequently printed and you'd like to remove things like sidebars from the printed page.

Media type defaults to `all`, so when you don't explicitly call a media type, for instance, `screen`, it will default to target screens (mobile screens, desktop screens, and so on) anyway.

There isn't a lot of knowledge available on the `speech`, `braille`, and `aural` media types at this point (they seem more like preparation material for the W3C's vision of the accessible future of the web), but for now you can use `display: none` on extraneous content that would make a screen reader repeat redundant content on various pages (like a logo's `alt` text) to help a visually impaired user access the actual content of the page.

You'll only use media type queries for fringe cases or if you're the type of web designer who consistently goes above and beyond client expectations to make sure that every single device functions amazingly—the downside being this kind of attention to detail is incredibly hard to maintain.

To avoid confusion and to put it simply, don't be swayed into thinking media types like `handheld` will consistently target what you're looking for. Instead, just target vaguely without media types. For instance:

```
@media (max-width: 700px) { … }
```

Is better than:

```
@media handheld { … }
```

Logical operators

You can use `and`, `not`, and `only` with media queries to achieve even more control. You can even concatenate conditions with commas, which is equivalent to the `or` operator. An example of a logical operator in place would be:

```
@media (min-width: 500px) and (max-width: 700px) {
    body {
        background: yellow;
    }
}
```

It will render a page that the body background color will change to yellow only between 500 px and 700 px.

A more useful example would be targeting an iPhone's orientation to display or hide a login form:

```
@media (max-width: 320px) and (orientation: portrait) {
    form.login {
        display: none;
    }
}
```

 We target the iPhone by using its width and also specify the orientation in case someone is using an even smaller phone on landscape.

Naturally, you could replace `and` with `not` and also `portrait` with `landscape` for the same effect; so the logical operators are pretty interchangeable. Just use whatever works best for the way you think logically.

You'll see a lot of code examples scattered around the Internet that use a lot of extraneous code. For instance, here is a popular snippet used to target iPad's in `portrait` mode:

```
@media only screen and (min-device-width: 768px) and
    (max-device-width: 1024px) and (orientation: portrait) {
    body {
        background: orange;
    }
}
```

 `device-width` will specify that this is exclusively used for devices, which is essentially any mobile device. To see how this works on your desktop, simply remove `-device` from each operator.

Essentially, we're only targeting non-desktop devices that are between 768 px and 1024 px in portrait mode. That is, only iPad tablets in portrait mode.

It's nice we have that kind of power, but this kind of targeting raises some concerns. We are almost literally only targeting iPads in portrait mode. Shouldn't desktop monitors at 800 x 600 resolutions get the same kind of usable rearrangement of elements? Why are we cutting off our media query for people below 768 px? Should we be using `device-width` at all? Why not just use `width`? Why are we specifying `screen`? As a developer, you should always try to remove as much cruft from your code as you can to make your code as flexible as possible. While having the power to target so radically is nice, it's also completely unnecessary and perhaps even hindering.

A much better approach to this situation would be to simply say, "When any device sees my site below 1024 px, I want my layout to rearrange to provide them with a nice experience. Once the width of the device falls to phone territory, I want to change it again."

```
@media (max-width: 1024px) {
    body {
        background: orange;
    }
}
@media (max-width: 768px) {
    body {
        background: yellow;
    }
}
```

 When any device hits 1024 px width, change the background color to orange; when it drops below that (into mobile territory), change the background to yellow.

Using this kind of degradation, we're able to serve a much wider array of devices with a fraction of the code. This is much more flexible. Not only is this faster and easier, but do you see how being vague with your media queries is a real strength?

In summary, media queries can be extremely powerful, but best used as vaguely as you can—all that strength and nothing to do with it.

In our next section we'll get into some really exciting stuff including the different approaches you'll encounter while making responsive websites.

Different strategies to make responsive websites

Since *Ethan Marcotte* coined the term "responsive web design", people have been looking for the best way to do it, which has cumulated into the Goldilocks approach versus the Fluid approach, and Desktop-first versus Mobile-first. The only right answer is to do what you're most comfortable with and, as always, avoid dogma. In this section we'll go over the differences between each approach and even sample them so your RWD tool belt is well equipped.

The Goldilocks approach

In 2011, and in response to the dilemma of building several iterations of the same website by targeting every single device, the web-design agency, Design by Front, came out with an official set of guidelines many designers were already adhering to. In essence, the Goldilocks approach states that rather than rearranging our layouts for every single device, we shouldn't be afraid of margins on the left and right of our designs. There's a blurb about sizing around the width of our body text (which they state should be around 66 characters per line, or 33 em's wide), but the important part is that they completely destroyed the train of thought that every single device needed to be explicitly targeted—effectively saving designers countless hours of time.

This approach became so prevalent that most CSS frameworks, including Twitter Bootstrap 2, adopted it without realizing that it had a name.

So how does this work exactly? You can see a demo at `http://goldilocksapproach.com/demo`; but for all you bathroom readers out there, you basically wrap your entire site in an element (or just target the body selector if it doesn't break anything else) and set the width of that element to something smaller than the width of the screen while applying a `margin: auto`.

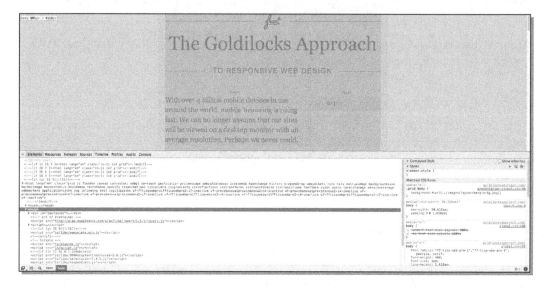

The highlighted element is the body tag. You can see the standard and huge margins on each side of it on larger desktop monitors.

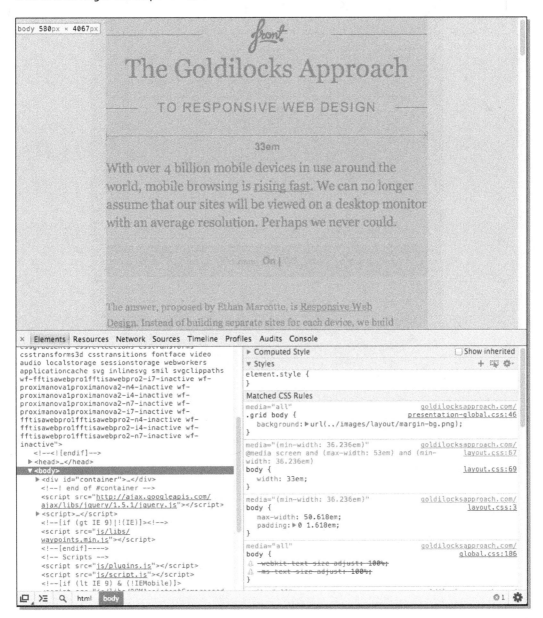

As you contract the viewport to a generic tablet-portrait size, you can see the width of the body is decreased dramatically, creating margins on each side again. They also do a little bit of rearranging by dropping the sidebar below the headline.

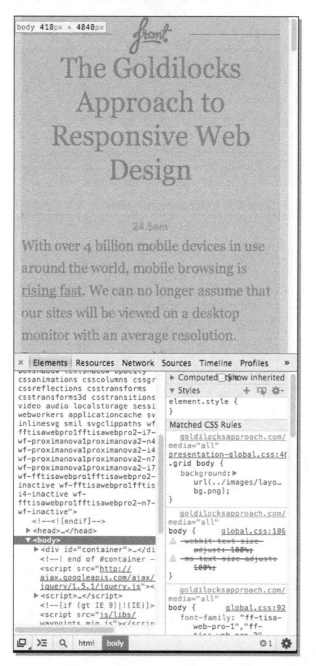

As you contract the viewport more to a phone size, you'll notice that the body of the page occupies the full width of the page now, with just some small margins on each side to keep text from butting up against the viewport edges.

Okay, so what are the advantages and disadvantages?

Well, one advantage is it's incredibly easy to do. You literally create a wrapping element and every time the width of the viewport touches the edges of that element, you make that element smaller and tweak a few things. But, the huge advantage is that you aren't targeting every single device, so you only have to write a small amount of code to make your site responsive.

The downside is that you're wasting a lot of screen real-estate with all those margins.

For the sake of practice, create a new folder called `Goldilocks`. Inside that folder create a `goldilocks.html` and `goldilocks.css` file. Put the following code in your `goldilocks.html` file:

```
<!DOCTYPE html>
<html>
    <head>
        <title>The Goldilocks Approach</title>
        <link rel="stylesheet" href="goldilocks.css">
    </head>
    <body>

        <div id="wrap">

            <header>
                <h1>The Goldilocks Approach</h1>
            </header>

            <section>
                <aside>Sidebar</aside>
                <article>
                    <header>
                        <h2>Hello World</h2>
                        <p>
                            Lorem ipsum...
                        </p>
                    </header>
                </article>
            </section>

        </div>

    </body>
</html>
```

We're creating an incredibly simple page with a header, sidebar, and content area to demonstrate how the Goldilocks approach works.

In your `goldilocks.css` file, put the following code:

```
* {
    margin: 0;
    padding: 0;
    background: rgba(0,0,0,.05);
    font: 13px/21px Arial, sans-serif;
}
h1, h2 {
    line-height: 1.2;
}
h1 {
    font-size: 30px;
}
h2 {
    font-size: 20px;
}
#wrap {
    width: 900px;
    margin: auto;
}
section {
    overflow: hidden;
}
aside {
    float: left;
    margin-right: 20px;
    width: 280px;
}
article {
    float: left;
    width: 600px;
}
@media (max-width: 900px) {
    #wrap {
        width: 500px;
    }
    aside {
        width: 180px;
    }
    article {
        width: 300px;
    }
}
```

```
@media (max-width: 500px) {
    #wrap {
        width: 96%;
        margin: 0 2%;
    }
    aside, article {
        width: 100%;
        margin-top: 10px;
    }
}
```

 Did you notice how the width of the #wrap element becomes the max-width of the media query?

After you save and refresh your page, you'll be able to expand/contract to your heart's content and enjoy your responsive website built with the Goldilocks approach. Look at you! You just made a site that will serve any device with only a few media queries. The fewer media queries you can get away with, the better!

Here's what it should look like:

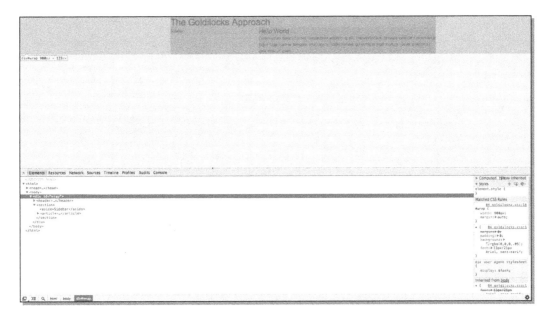

The preceding screenshot shows your Goldilocks page at desktop width. At tablet size, it looks like the following:

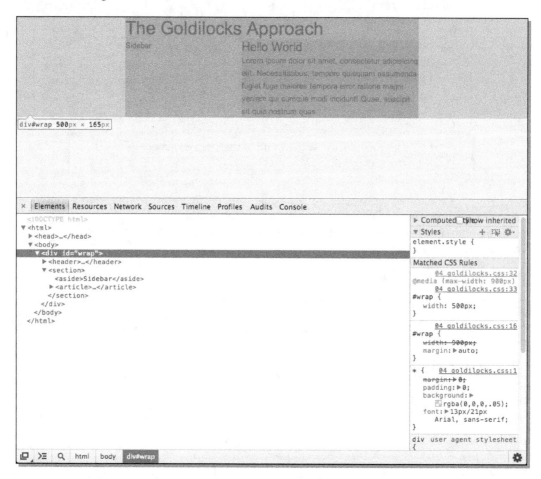

On a mobile site, you should see something like the following screenshot:

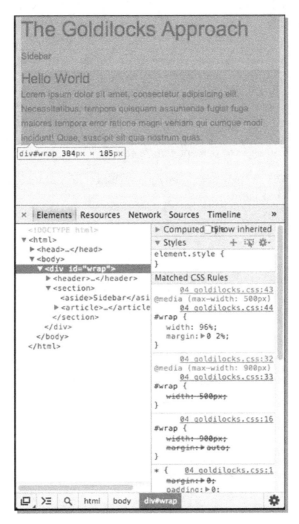

The Goldilocks approach is great for websites that are graphic heavy as you can convert just three mockups to layouts and have completely custom, graphic-rich websites that work on almost any device. It's nice if you are of the type who enjoys spending a lot of time in Photoshop and don't mind putting in the extra work of recreating a lot of code for a more textured website with a lot of attention to detail.

The Fluid approach

Loss of real estate and a substantial amount of extra work for slightly prettier (and heavier) websites is a problem that most of us don't want to deal with. We still want beautiful sites, and luckily with pure CSS, we can replicate a huge amount of elements in flexible code. A common, real-world example of replacing images with CSS is to use CSS to create buttons.

Where Goldilocks looks at your viewport as a container for smaller, usually pixel-based containers, the Fluid approach looks at your viewport as a 100 percent large container. If every element inside the viewport adds up to around 100 percent, you've effectively used the real estate you were given.

Duplicate your `goldilocks.html` file, then rename it to `fluid.html`. Replace the mentions of `"Goldilocks"` with `"Fluid"`:

```
<!DOCTYPE html>
<html>
    <head>
        <title>The Fluid Approach</title>
        <link rel="stylesheet" href="fluid.css">
    </head>
    <body>

        <div id="wrap">

            <header>
                <h1>The Fluid Approach</h1>
            </header>

            <section>
                <aside>Sidebar</aside>
                <article>
                    <header>
                        <h2>Hello World</h2>
                    </header>
        <p>
                        Lorem ipsum...
                    </p>
                </article>
            </section>

        </div>

    </body>
</html>
```

 We're just duplicating our very simple header, sidebar, and article layout.

Create a `fluid.css` file and put the following code in it:

```
* {
    margin: 0;
    padding: 0;
    background: rgba(0,0,0,.05);
    font: 13px/21px Arial, sans-serif;
}
aside {
    float: left;
    width: 24%;
    margin-right: 1%;
}
article {
    float: left;
    width: 74%;
    margin-left: 1%;
}
```

[Wow! That's a lot less code already.]

Save and refresh your browser, then expand/contract your viewport. Did you notice how we're using all available space? Did you notice how we didn't even have to use media queries and it's already responsive? Percentages are pretty cool.

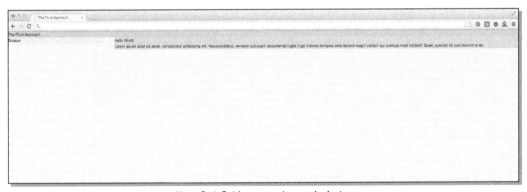

Your first fluid, responsive, web design

We have a few problems though:

- ✦ On large monitors, when that layout is full of text, every paragraph will fit on one line. That's horrible for readability.

- ✦ Text and other elements butt up against the edges of the design.

- ✦ The sidebar and article, although responsive, don't look great on smaller devices. They're too small.

Luckily, these are all pretty easy fixes. First, let's make sure the layout of our content doesn't stretch to 100 percent of the width of the viewport when we're looking at it in larger resolutions. To do this, we use a CSS property called `max-width`.

Append the following code to your `fluid.css` file:

```
#wrap {
    max-width: 980px;
    margin: auto;
}
```

What do you think `max-width` does?

Save and refresh, expand and contract. You'll notice that wrapping `div` is now centered in the screen at 980 px width, but what happens when you go below 980 px? It simply converts to 100 percent width. This isn't the only way you'll use `max-width`, but we'll learn a bit more in the *Gotchas and best practices* section.

Our second problem was that the elements were butting up against the edges of the screen. This is an easy enough fix. You can either wrap everything in another element with specified margins on the left and right, or simply add some padding to our `#wrap` element shown as follows:

```
#wrap {
    max-width: 980px;
    margin: auto;
    padding: 0 20px;
}
```

Now our text and other elements are touching the edges of the viewport.

Finally, we need to rearrange the layout for smaller devices, so our sidebar and article aren't so tiny. To do this, we'll have to use a media query and simply unassign the properties we defined in our original CSS:

```
@media (max-width: 600px) {
    aside, article {
        float: none;
        width: 100%;
        margin: 10px 0;
    }
}
```

We're removing the float because it's unnecessary, giving these elements a width of 100 percent, and removing the left and right margins while adding some margins on the top and bottom so that we can differentiate the elements.

This act of moving elements on top of each other like this is known as stacking.

Simple enough, right? We were able to make a really nice, real-world, responsive, fluid layout in just 28 lines of CSS.

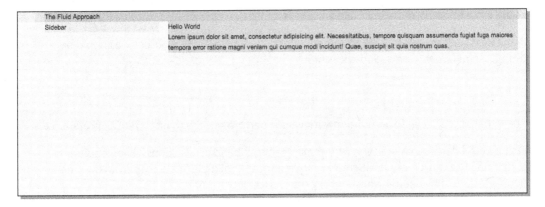

On smaller devices, we stack content areas to help with readability/usability:

> **The Fluid Approach**
>
> Sidebar
>
> Hello World
> Lorem ipsum dolor sit amet, consectetur adipisicing elit.
> Necessitatibus, tempore quisquam assumenda fugiat fuga
> maiores tempora error ratione magni veniam qui cumque modi
> incidunt! Quae, suscipit sit quia nostrum quas.

It's up to you how you want to design your websites. If you're a huge fan of lush graphics and don't mind doing extra work or wasting real estate, then use Goldilocks. I used Goldilocks for years until I noticed a beautiful site with only one breakpoint (width-based media query), then I switched to Fluid and haven't looked back.

It's entirely up to you. I'd suggest you make a few websites using Goldilocks, get a bit annoyed at the extra effort, then try out Fluid and see if it fits.

In the next section we'll talk about a somewhat new debate about whether we should be designing for larger or smaller devices first.

Desktop-first versus Mobile-first

The debate boils down to amount of work versus performance with just a hint of preference.

On powerful desktop computers, with their nice broadband connections, downloading something like the jQuery JavaScript library is almost negligible. It's so common that many people include it by default whether they make a lot of use it or not.

At the time of this writing, a minified copy of jQuery clocks in at around 84 KB. That's not a huge factor until you're downloading that from your dinky 3G smart phone while cutting into and out of single. Then it can be excruciating and even turn a lot of users away. How many times have you become frustrated at how slow a site was loading on your phone and started violently mashing your screen trying to get some response out of it?

The Mobile-first camp states that we should leave everything we possibly can, out (JavaScript libraries, media, fancy stuff) and only add it when it's absolutely necessary, or replace it where possible. This dramatically cuts down on page load times, but, as with any optimization, it requires more effort.

The Desktop-first camp states that since the majority of users browse the Internet on desktop computers (although there's some debate even about this), we should all design rich experiences with desktops in mind and just provide the bare minimum experience for mobile users.

As *Joshua Johnson* writes in his blog post, *Mobile First Design: Why It's Great and Why It Sucks...*

> *Let's look for a second at my arguments for and against a mobile first design approach. In the for category, we have straightforward and logical arguments that are difficult to downplay. In the against category, I have a lot of whining and personal hesitation. Which side do you think wins this battle?*

The battle can be summed up as graceful degradation (Desktop-first) versus progressive enhancement (Mobile-first), only the degradation isn't always graceful.

Desktop-first

So far we've only been working with the Desktop-first approach. A tell-tale sign that you're approaching the subject from a Desktop-first angle is our media queries. Notice they are all `max-width`. Mobile-first tends to lean towards `min-width`.

We've been working with Desktop-first to avoid confusion, and because I believe most of you are following along with a large monitor—hardly anyone develops on a tablet or mobile device.

As we've already made a few sites using the Desktop-first approach, there isn't really a need to recreate another, but as an exercise, browse the CSS (you may need to run it through a CSS beautifier) on some of the responsive sites found at `http://mediaqueri.es` and see which ones were made with a Desktop-first approach. Most responsive sites are, but that's just because Mobile-first is relatively new in comparison. As time goes on, I suspect more and more sites will be Mobile-first.

Mobile-first

The major points to consider while making your site Mobile-first are:

✦ JavaScript load
✦ CSS load
✦ Image load

Think about what is actually happening with your JavaScript. Is it a library? If so, do you need it on every page? Are you just making an alert box? Do you need to even load a library? Could you write that alert box script in pure JavaScript?

By going through that simple checklist you can get rid of a huge chunk of scripts and optimize your site for all devices. What if you really want a script for desktop but not for mobile? There's a way around that. A site called `detectmobilebrowsers.com` provides you with code in various languages to detect whether or not the user is on a mobile device. If they are, it typically returns true. With that knowledge, you can choose to load or not to load the script.

This is a finicky fix though. This script will need maintenance by someone, so that it is able to detect newer and newer browser agents. It seems to target everything now, but perhaps in the future, you'll have to maintain your own script. The other problem with this particular script is that the actual pure JavaScript function doesn't return a variable as true or false, it simply redirects to another page. Serving various sites dependent on a device is not responsive. In fact, it's very anti-responsive.

Let's modify the code a bit so that we get a simple true or false value if the agent is a mobile device: `https://gist.github.com/CorySimmons/6140696`.

Create a file called `detect.js` and save the Gist above to it. Hang on to that.

With this updated code, we can now use the `isMobile` variable to detect if the user is on a mobile browser. Nice! Let's jump right into making our first Mobile-first site.

Create a new file called `mobile-first.html` and add the following:

```
<!DOCTYPE html>
<html>
    <head>
        <title>Mobile First</title>
        <link rel="stylesheet" href="mobile-first.css">
    </head>
    <body>

        <div id="wrap">

            <header>
                <h1>Mobile First</h1>
            </header>

            <section>
                <aside>Sidebar</aside>
                <article>
                    <header>
                        <h2>Hello World</h2>
                    </header>
                    <p>
                        Lorem ipsum...
                    </p>
                </article>
```

```
        </section>

    </div>

    <script src="detect.js"></script>
    <script src="http://rkitover.github.com/
      load-js/load.js"></script>
    <script>
        if(isMobile == false) {
            load_jquery();
        }
    </script>
    <script>
        if(isMobile == false) {
            $('header').css('background', 'blue');
        }
    </script>

    </body>
</html>
```

We've added a `load.js` script that will make it possible to load CSS and JS within `<script>` blocks.

You'll notice `detect.js` is doing its job. It's detecting if the user is on a mobile browser, if they aren't, it sets `isMobile` to `false`. After that, we're using a neat, lightweight, script called `load.js` (`https://github.com/rkitover/load-js`) written by *Rafael Kitover* to load CSS and JS within a `<script>` block. That JS isn't available until the next `<script>` block, so we need to create a new `<script>` block and repeat our `isMobile` test to make sure we're not trying to use jQuery when it's not available.

Upload `mobile-first.html` to your web host and navigate to it. On desktops and laptops your headers should be blue as set by jQuery; on mobile devices, they will not be blue.

Let's review. We're loading a small `detect.js` script and the small `load.js` for every visitor. This detects if they are on a mobile device. If so, we don't load anything. If they aren't on a mobile device, we load and execute some jQuery.

There are a myriad of ways to load/not load JavaScript and it can get pretty abstract, but this is a great way for Mobile-first beginners to jump right in and see some massive savings on mobile page load time.

Back to the fun stuff! Create a file called `mobile-first.css` and add the following:

```css
* {
    margin: 0;
    padding: 0;
    background: rgba(0,0,0,.05);
    font: 13px/21px Arial, sans-serif;
}
#wrap {
    max-width: 980px;
    margin: auto;
    padding: 0 20px;
}
aside, article {
    margin: 10px 0;
}
@media (min-width: 600px) {
    aside {
        float: left;
        width: 24%;
        margin-right: 1%;
    }
    article {
        float: left;
        width: 74%;
        margin-left: 1%;
    }
}
```

Notice that we're using `min-width` now instead of `max-width`.

Does this code look familiar? It should, it's just `fluid.css` rearranged a bit.

 If you can make Desktop-first sites, you can rearrange the code a bit and turn it into a Mobile-first site fairly easily.

Notice it's a bit (two lines) smaller? That's because we're not overriding any CSS. We're building on the defaults. As the page grows, we morph our layout into something that looks better on desktops. We're progressively enhancing.

Save `mobile-first.css` and refresh `mobile-first.html`, expand and contract. Looks just like `fluid.html`, doesn't it? Except this time around, it's a bit faster. Two lines may not seem like much, but by using this approach you can eliminate hundreds, if not thousands (for bigger sites), of CSS that was before being rendered, then overwritten and re-rendered. This can make for some pretty big page load optimizations especially on mobile devices.

Finally, you should consider images. Images that are too big can make all your other efforts completely worthless, but we need images right? Well, maybe!

We can eliminate a lot of imagery altogether with some nice CSS. For instance, there are a countless number of CSS button generators out there. One of the more interesting projects is `layerstyles.org`, where you can effectively replicate the Photoshop Layers palette, create custom elements, and grab the CSS. Naturally, as you get better, you won't need fun tools like this. You might even replace them with some incredibly efficient CSS preprocessor mixings, but that's a book for another day. The point is, CSS has come a long way and you don't need nearly as many images as you'd think. Replace as many images with CSS as possible for the easiest/largest savings.

Here's a quick CSS button:

```
.button {
    background: #f13c3c;
    color: #fff;
    text-shadow: 0 1px 1px #dd2a2a;
    border-radius: 3px;
    border: 1px solid #dd2a2a;
    box-shadow: inset 0 1px 0 0 #f76666;
    padding: 10px 30px;
    text-decoration: none;
    display: inline-block;
    margin: 10px 0;
}
```

Any element with the .button class applied to it will look like a button. See how flexible these are?

Naturally, you can't get rid of every image. You'll have logos and such. The solutions for these situations range from serving a small image and using JavaScript to detect if the user is on a desktop and replacing the `src` attribute with a larger version of the same image, to things as complex as editing your Apache configuration to do something similar, to even wrapping every image in a `<noscript>` tag with data attributes and writing a chunk of JavaScript to add and size imagery.

These solutions are constantly evolving. Since *Ethan Marcotte* coined the term "responsive web design" a few years ago, there have been dozens of independently developed solutions and it seems like a new standard is coming out every other day.

To go over them all, or to pick one from the batch, would escape the scope of this book and probably be outdated by the time you get this far, but if you're particularly interested in these page load savings, check out a fairly thorough article on the topic written by Jason Grigsby at `http://blog.cloudfour.com/responsive-imgs-part-2`.

In short, and to avoid confusion, just use as few images as possible. This is a huge reason for the current "flat" (Google Flat UI) trend in web design. It's clean, fast, and doesn't burden the developer with having to maintain multiple image sizes and huge chunks of code just to serve images.

It's entirely up to you whether you prefer a Desktop or Mobile-first approach, but the data and most experts agree that Mobile-first is the wave of the future so it would definitely behoove an aspiring web designer to at least become familiar with developing Mobile-first websites.

In the next section we'll cover some common and strange behavior that might cause you to freak out a bit. Particularly making images and video responsive, and pixel-sizing this may make your responsive sites, not-so-responsive.

Gotchas and best practices

Let's start with images. Grab a big image. If you need help, just search for Packt Publishing Logo and find one.

Once we have our image, let's duplicate our `mobile-first.html` page and call it `gotchas.html`. Go ahead and do the same with `mobile-first.css`, call it `gotchas.css`. Replace any references to `mobile-first[.html, .css]` with `gotchas[.html, .css]`.

The HTML:

```
<!DOCTYPE html>
<html>
    <head>
        <title>Gotchas</title>
        <link rel="stylesheet" href="gotchas.css">
    </head>
    <body>

        <div id="wrap">

            <header>
                <h1>Gotchas</h1>
            </header>

            <section>
```

```
                    <aside>Sidebar</aside>
                    <article>
                        <header>
                            <h2>Hello World</h2>
                        </header>
                        <p>
                            Lorem ipsum...
                        </p>
                    </article>
                </section>

            </div>

            <script src="detect.js"></script>
            <script src="http://rkitover.github.com/
              load-js/load.js"></script>
            <script>
                if(isMobile == false) {
                    load_jquery();
                }
            </script>
            <script>
                if(isMobile == false) {
                    $('header').css('background', 'blue');
                }
            </script>

    </body>
</html>
* {
    margin: 0;
    padding: 0;
    background: rgba(0,0,0,.05);
    font: 13px/21px Arial, sans-serif;
}
#wrap {
    max-width: 980px;
    margin: auto;
    padding: 0 20px;
}
aside, article {
    margin: 10px 0;
}
@media (min-width: 600px) {
    aside {
        float: left;
        width: 24%;
        margin-right: 1%;
    }
    article {
```

```
        float: left;
        width: 74%;
        margin-left: 1%;
    }
}
```

The CSS:

Now replace `<h1>Gotchas</h1>` with `<figure class="logo"><img src="packtpub.jpg"></figure>`. Save and refresh. Whoa! That's too big!

Fret not! Quickly open your `gotchas.css` file and append the following:

```
.logo {
    width: 30%;
}
.logo img {
    max-width: 100%;
}
```

I told you we'd see `max-width` again!

So what's going on here? We're setting the image's wrapping element to a width of 30 percent of its 980 px wide container and the image itself to fill that wrapping element. In effect, it makes our image constantly conform to be 30 percent of `#wrap`, even as it shrinks below 980 px.

Can't we just do this?

```
.logo img {
    width: 30%;
}
```

Well, yes; it will work as expected, but do you want to have to specify every image you ever use to be a certain size or would you rather just have the image fill its container by default no matter how big or small? Keep in mind, if you use a small image inside a big container, it will stretch the image and you'll lose resolution—hence, I asked you to find a big image for this exercise. In such instances, feel free to specify the width of the image as auto so that it doesn't stretch.

This strategy is so common it has become a standard in the world of RWD—standardized by the pioneer of RWD itself, Ethan Marcotte. In short, if you're having issues with images not sizing properly, just apply the size you want, to their wrapping element, and then give them a `max-width` of `100%`. It's not uncommon to see the following code in a CSS reset:

```
img {
    max-width: 100%;
}
```

 Just make sure images are always wrapped in an element with a defined size, and it's large enough to shrink down to fit whatever container it's in.

This is the easiest way, but again, you have to be careful about dumping too many images into your site and burdening the casual mobile user with huge load times. I can typically get by with a couple of images, a logo and a background image, so it's not a huge issue. Just be extremely mindful when you notice you're using more than two to three rather large images on a single page.

This strategy is supposed to work on video as well, but as with most things in CSS, it's never that easy. This brings us to our next gotcha videos.

There is huge article written by *Thierry Koblentz*, on A List Apart, titled *Creating Intrinsic Ratios for Video*, that covers this topic in depth, but who wants to read all that? Not to mention the finalized code for doing this correctly is immense.

Luckily Chris Coyier (CSS Tricks) and Dave Rupert (Paravel) made a JavaScript plugin that makes this incredibly easy called FitVids. Read about it at `https://github.com/davatron5000/FitVids.js`.

Go find a YouTube video you like, grab the embed code under the Share link, save a copy of `FitVids.js` to your project directory, and modify your `gotchas.html` file shown as follows:

```
<!DOCTYPE html>
<html>
    <head>
        <title>Gotchas</title>
        <link rel="stylesheet" href="gotchas.css">
    </head>
```

```
<body>

    <div id="wrap">

        <header>
            <figure class="logo"><img
              src="packtpub.jpg"></figure>
        </header>

        <section>
            <aside>Sidebar</aside>
            <article>
                <header>
                    <h2>Hello World</h2>
                </header>
                <p>
                    Lorem ipsum...
                </p>

                <div class="video_wrapper">
                    <iframe width="960" height="720" src="http://
www.youtube.com/embed/FR7wOGyAzpw" frameborder="0" allowfullscreen></
iframe>
                </div>

            </article>
        </section>

    </div>

    <script src="http://ajax.googleapis.com/ajax/libs/
jquery/1.10.2/jquery.min.js"></script>
    <script src="jquery.fitvids.js"></script>
    <script>
        $('.video_wrapper').fitVids();
    </script>

</body>
</html>
```

 Notice we're explicitly specifying the HTTP protocol of the URLs to be http, rather than leaving them blank, this way we can test locally.

FitVids.js relies on jQuery, so the steps are:

✦ Place embedded code in a wrapping element; in this case, .video_wrapper

✦ Import jQuery (in this case we're importing from Google's CDN)

✦ Import FitVids

✦ Apply the fitVids() function to whatever selectors match your video wrapping elements

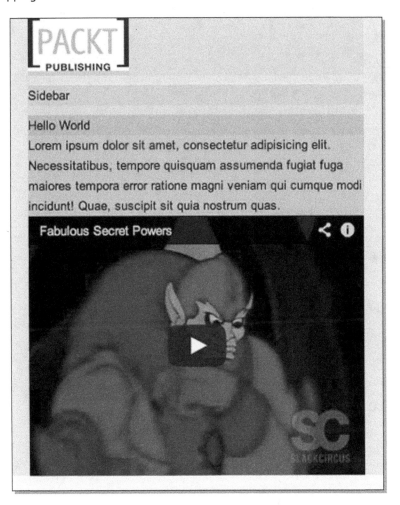

The last thing we're going to cover in the gotchas section is the `viewport` meta tag. To put this in the least confusing way possible, a pixel can be various sizes on various devices. By default, and if you've been viewing your responsive sites on your phone this entire time and wondering why they aren't stacking, it's because the browser is interpreting the viewport incorrectly which in practice, turns your responsive site into a desktop site.

It's basically trying to guess as to what you were trying to do, which is fine for unresponsive sites, but for those of us who are working their butts off to make nice, responsive sites, it's a pain in the neck. Luckily, it's an incredibly easy fix. Add the following to the `<head>` of `gotchas.html`:

```
<meta name="viewport" content="width=device-width, initial-scale=1">
```

 Now your device's viewport will interpret pixels literally, which will in-turn activate your media queries.

For more information on the specifics of the `viewport` meta tag, search for The Idiot's Guide to Viewport and Pixel.

Putting it all together

We're drawing to the end. You've been a good student. Let's have fun actually creating a real, responsive website.

Get your typing fingers ready...

Create a new file called `instant.html`, fill with the following code:

```
<!DOCTYPE html>
<html>
    <head>
        <title>INSTANT Responsive Web-Design</title>
        <meta name="viewport" content="width=device-width,
          initial-scale=1">
        <link rel="stylesheet" href="instant.css">
    </head>
    <body>

        <header class="top">
            <div class="center">

                <figure class="logo"><img
                  src="packtpub.png"></figure>

                <nav>
                    <a href="#">Link</a>
                    <a href="#">Link</a>
```

```
                    <a href="#">Link</a>
                    <a href="#">Link</a>
                </nav>

            </div>
        </header>

        <section class="main">
            <div class="center">

                <aside>
                    <nav>
                        <a href="#">Sublink</a>
                        <a href="#">Sublink</a>
                        <a href="#">Sublink</a>
                        <a href="#">Sublink</a>
                        <a href="#">Sublink</a>
                        <a href="#">Sublink</a>
                    </nav>
                </aside>
                <article>
                    <header>
                        <h2>INSTANT Responsive Web-Design</h2>
                    </header>
                    <p>
                        Lorem ipsum...
                    </p>
                    <div class="video_wrapper">
                        <iframe width="960" height="720" src="http://
www.youtube.com/embed/FR7wOGyAzpw" frameborder="0" allowfullscreen></
iframe>
                    </div>
                </article>

            </div>
        </section>

        <script src="http://ajax.googleapis.com/ajax/libs/
jquery/1.10.2/jquery.min.js"></script>
        <script src="jquery.fitvids.js"></script>
        <script>
            $('.video_wrapper').fitVids();
        </script>

    </body>
</html>
```

Where'd #wrap go?

We've added some classes to our first header element and our section element. We've also replaced the #wrap element with <div class="center">. This way we can set full width backgrounds and still have our background-less content centered all the same.

Create a file called instant.css and insert the following code:

```css
* {
    margin: 0;
    padding: 0;
    font: 13px/21px Arial, sans-serif;
}
html {
    background: #2ecc71;
}
img {
    max-width: 100%;
}
.top {
    background: #34495e;
    overflow: hidden;
}
.logo {
    width: 50%;
    margin: 20px auto;
}
.top nav {
    margin-bottom: 10px;
    overflow: hidden;
}
.top nav a {
    background: #ecf0f1;
    text-align: center;
    text-decoration: none;
    border-radius: 5px;
    padding: 10px 0;
    color: #34495e;
    font-weight: bold;
    margin: 10px auto;
    width: 90%;
    display: block;
}
aside nav a {
    display: block;
    text-decoration: none;
    text-align: center;
    padding: 10px 0;
    background: #ecf0f1;
    color: #075227;
```

```
        font-weight: bold;
        border-bottom: 1px solid #ddd;
}
h2 {
        font-size: 30px;
        font-weight: bold;
        margin-bottom: 10px;
        line-height: 1.2;
        text-align: center;
}
p {
        margin-bottom: 20px;
}
article {
        background: #ecf0f1;
        margin: 15px;
        border-radius: 5px;
        padding: 15px;
}

@media (min-width: 600px) {
        aside {
                float: left;
                width: 25%;
        }
        article {
                float: left;
                width: 69%;
                padding: 3%;
        }
        .center {
                max-width: 980px;
                margin: auto;
                padding: 0 20px;
        }
        .logo {
                float: left;
                width: 20%;
                padding: 20px 0;
                margin-right: 10%;
        }
        .top nav {
                float: left;
                width: 70%;
                margin-top: 60px;
        }
        .top nav a {
                float: left;
```

```
        width: 23%;
        margin-left: 1%;
        margin-right: 1%;
    }
    .top nav a:first-child {
        width: 24%;
        margin-left: 0;
    }
    .top nav a:last-child {
        width: 24%;
        margin-right: 0;
    }
    aside nav a {
        margin-bottom: 10px;
        border-radius: 5px;
        border-top-right-radius: 0;
        border-bottom-right-radius: 0;
    }
    .main {
        overflow: hidden;
        padding-top: 30px;
    }
    article {
        margin: 0;
        padding: 3%;
        border-radius: 0;
        border-top-right-radius: 5px;
        border-bottom-right-radius: 5px;
        border-bottom-left-radius: 5px;
    }
    h2 {
        text-align: left;
    }
}
```

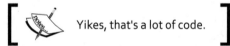

Yikes, that's a lot of code.

Remember, things that will stay the same (background colors, fonts, and so on) should go outside of the media query in this Mobile-first approach. The only things that go inside of the media query have to do with the layout, and desktop-specific styling (rounded corners, and so on).

The process of doing this goes something like:

- ✦ Create mobile version that looks nice
- ✦ Add a `min-width` media query
- ✦ Add desktop-specific styling in that media query
- ✦ Tweak, tweak, tweak

Desktop view of our mobile-first site

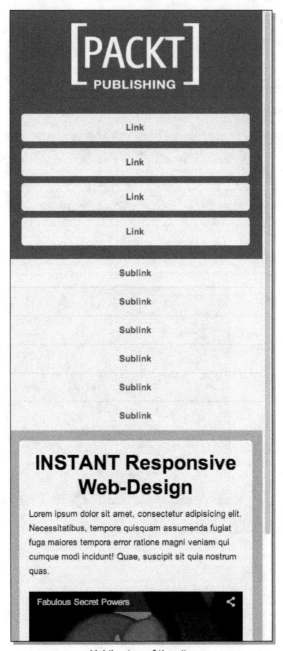

Mobile view of the site

Nice! Kudos! You're a responsive guru now! Well, not entirely, but after you build a couple of sites with these practices in mind, you'll be well on your way.

If you start feeling like you're repeating styles, especially in regards to your layouts, buttons, forms, and so on, you should definitely check out the insanely vast plethora of responsive CSS frameworks out there including Bootstrap, Foundation, and Inuit.

Still not enough for your hungry mind? Learn about the CSS preprocessors: LESS, SASS/SCSS, and Stylus. There are some really clever tools out there that will do things like generate responsive grids and buttons for you on the fly. Some notable ones are Bourbon Neat (great spacing between nested columns), `Singularity.gs` (insane), and even one written by yours truly called Jeet (`http://jeetframework.com`), which will let you specify column widths with any fraction. It's also packed with all the bells and whistles needed to make converting an idea into a responsive website a cakewalk.

Frameworks and preprocessors can be a bit tricky to get comfortable with, but don't give up hope, the payoffs are huge. I can literally recreate the same `instant.html` file in about five minutes from scratch using a framework and preprocessor.

People and places you should get to know

There are so many contributors to the RWD world that it's hard to narrow down a few, but the ones I follow most are:

- ✦ Ethan Marcotte, the RWD pioneer (`http://ethanmarcotte.com`)
- ✦ Luke Wroblewski, the Mobile-first pioneer (`http://lukew.com`)
- ✦ Brad Frost, a Mobile-first fanatic (`http://bradfrostweb.com`)
- ✦ Harry Roberts, whose well-written CSS articles can be found at `http://csswizardry.com`
- ✦ Chris Coyier, who always tackles CSS problems (`http://css-tricks.com`)
- ✦ Mark Otto and Jacob Thornton, the Twitter Bootstrap creators (`@mdo` and `@fat`)

As with everything, the best place to find information about RWD is Google, but some sites that often pop up in my search results are `www.html5rocks.com` and `www.alistapart.com`.

Also, be sure to get an IRC client and go to the `www.freenode.net` server and `#css` channel. Freenode is a gold mine of incredibly helpful gurus, but don't abuse it. It will be obvious if you haven't searched for an answer or if you're trying to get someone to write all the code for you. Be very polite, ask questions, provide a bare bones example of your issue (use `jsfiddle.net` to create demos), and answer questions once you get better. The more IRC credit you have, the faster you'll get meaningful, educational, and help from it.

StackOverflow is full of questions about responsive design that have already been thoroughly answered, so I suggest you to use Google to do a site search of StackOverflow (for example, `site:stackoverflow.com responsive video`) for answers to your questions before bothering the nice folks at IRC.

I hope you have learned a lot from this book. You now know the different approaches to RWD and the important gotchas. Go off into the world my pupils! Create beautiful, usable, websites, and get fat stacks!

Feel free to follow me on Twitter at `@ccccory`—I'm pretty cool, my mom tells me so.

Thank you for buying
Instant Responsive Web Design

About Packt Publishing

Packt, pronounced 'packed', published its first book *"Mastering phpMyAdmin for Effective MySQL Management"* in April 2004 and subsequently continued to specialize in publishing highly focused books on specific technologies and solutions.

Our books and publications share the experiences of your fellow IT professionals in adapting and customizing today's systems, applications, and frameworks. Our solution based books give you the knowledge and power to customize the software and technologies you're using to get the job done. Packt books are more specific and less general than the IT books you have seen in the past. Our unique business model allows us to bring you more focused information, giving you more of what you need to know, and less of what you don't.

Packt is a modern, yet unique publishing company, which focuses on producing quality, cutting-edge books for communities of developers, administrators, and newbies alike. For more information, please visit our website: www.packtpub.com.

Writing for Packt

We welcome all inquiries from people who are interested in authoring. Book proposals should be sent to author@packtpub.com. If your book idea is still at an early stage and you would like to discuss it first before writing a formal book proposal, contact us; one of our commissioning editors will get in touch with you.

We're not just looking for published authors; if you have strong technical skills but no writing experience, our experienced editors can help you develop a writing career, or simply get some additional reward for your expertise.

PUBLISHING

Quick answers to common problems

HTML5 and CSS3 Responsive Web Design Cookbook

Learn the secrets of developing responsive websites capable of interfacing with today's mobile Internet devices

Benjamin LaGrone

HTML5 and CSS3 Responsive Web Design Cookbook

ISBN: 978-1-84969-544-2   Paperback: 204 pages

Learn the secrets of developing responsive websites capable of interfacing with today's mobile Internet devices

1. Learn the fundamental elements of writing responsive website code for all stages of the development lifecycle

2. Create the ultimate code writer's resource using logical workflow layers

3. Full of usable code for immediate use in your website projects

---

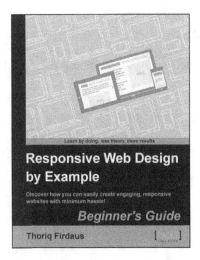

Learn by doing: less theory, more results

Responsive Web Design by Example

Discover how you can easily create engaging, responsive websites with minimum hassle!

Beginner's Guide

Thoriq Firdaus

Responsive Web Design by Example

ISBN: 978-1-84969-542-8   Paperback: 338 pages

Discover how you can easily create engaging, responsive websites with minimum hassle!

1. Rapidly develop and prototype responsive websites by utilizing powerful open source frameworks

2. Focus less on the theory and more on results, with clear step-by-step instructions, previews, and examples to help you along the way

3. Learn how you can utilize three of the most powerful responsive frameworks available today: Bootstrap, Skeleton, and Zurb Foundation

Please check **www.PacktPub.com** for information on our titles

Responsive Web Design with HTML5 and CSS3

ISBN: 978-1-84969-318-9   Paperback: 324 pages

Learn responsive design using HTML5 and CSS3 to adapt websites to any browser or screen size

1. Everything needed to code websites in HTML5 and CSS3 that are responsive to every device or screen size

2. Learn the main new features of HTML5 and use CSS3's stunning new capabilities including animations, transitions and transformations

3. Real world examples show how to progressively enhance a responsive design while providing fall backs for older browsers

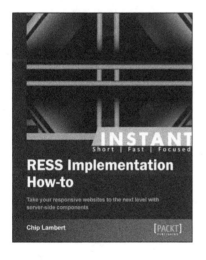

Instant RESS Implementation How-to [Instant]

ISBN: 978-1-84969-692-0   Paperback: 58 pages

Take your responsive websites to the next level with server-side components

1. Learn something new in an Instant! A short, fast, focused guide delivering immediate results

2. Build a dynamic website that reacts according to the device

3. Get started with the Modernizr JavaScript library for feature detection

Please check **www.PacktPub.com** for information on our titles